IMAGES
of America

SAN DIEGO POLICE
CASE FILES

Chief William Lansdowne began his law enforcement career in 1966 with the San Jose Police Department, where he steadily rose through the ranks to become assistant chief of police. Lansdowne then moved across the bay to head the Richmond California Police Department before returning to assume the top job within San Jose Police Department. After a nationwide search, Lansdowne beat out other contenders to take the job as San Diego Police Department (SDPD) chief in 2003.

ON THE COVER: Early-1950s television shows such as *Dragnet* created a strong public interest in law enforcement. Not wanting to miss out on the community-relations possibilities, San Diego television station KFSD partnered with the SDPD to create the show *Information Police*. Broadcast locally, Sgt. Bob Crosby was the host. The show was an informational series, with guests discussing a wide variety of topics, including police patrol procedures, how to call the police, personal safety, and other related issues.

IMAGES
of America

SAN DIEGO POLICE
CASE FILES

Steve Willard and Ed LaValle

ARCADIA
PUBLISHING

This book is dedicated to family, friends, and the 10,000 men and women who have worn a badge to serve America's finest city. We also honor the men and women of San Diego city law enforcement who paid the ultimate price in protecting our community.

CONTENTS

Acknowledgments

Acknowledgments can be exceptionally difficult. Invariably, something gets lost or we forget to mention a person's name. If that occurred here, no disrespect or lack of gratitude was intended.

Special thanks are due the following people: Our guest contributors from the San Diego Police Department are Chief William Lansdowne; executive assistant David Ramirez; Assistant Chiefs Boyd Long, Lawrence McKinney, Cesar Solis, and Shelley Zimmerman; crime lab director Jennifer Shen; Det. Gary Hassen; and Officers Scott Napora, War Lovell, Nicholas Nguyen, and Tony Zeljeznjak.

From the San Diego Police Museum, we thank the entire board of directors for their support of this project and authorization for the use of photographs, chief archivist Tom Giaquinto, and Commissioners Ramin Pourteymour and Norman "Skip" Sperber. Photographers Debbie Jezior and Tom Keck also deserve accolades.

From the general public, we would like to thank Charles Koer for submitting a number of great photographs taken during the distinguished career of his father, Jake. We thank all members of the San Diego Police Department, past and present. Without your dedication, there would be no story to tell.

Last, but certainly not least, it would be an understatement to say the museum would not exist without pioneering individuals such as Sgt. Edward W. Kenney and historian Pliney Castenian. Without them and the diligent archiving of materials and researching of facts, the San Diego Police Museum absolutely could not exist. Unless otherwise noted, all images are courtesy of the San Diego Police Historical Association.

INTRODUCTION

There are literally hundreds of thousands of case files that have been created in the 122 years of work by the San Diego Police Department. Even more files cover the work of the San Diego city marshals, the men tasked with keeping the peace until the 1889 formation of the San Diego Police Department (SDPD).

It is a challenge to articulate the overall content of those files and their role in San Diego's crime history. Some things are simply too much for one book, much less a photograph. This is why the San Diego Police Museum is so important: it is a centralized location to showcase the incredible history of a major city law enforcement agency. Equally important, the museum also houses the names of all San Diego city law enforcement officers who paid the ultimate price to protect our community.

Formed in 1997 from little more than just a good idea, the San Diego Police Historical Association, the parent agency of the police museum, has achieved a remarkable track record. First, we partnered with other community groups to save our largest historical artifact, the National Register of Historic Place Old Police Headquarters. Then we opened a museum for the public.

As we grew, so did our fleet of historical vehicles. Today, the association has America's largest fleet of historical police vehicles. Starting with a 1928 patrol car, each decade until modern times is represented by at least one fully functional car of the era. The flagship of our fleet is a 1932 Ford prisoner transportation wagon.

But that is only one part of the story. The San Diego Police Museum also holds the world's largest archive of SDPD badges, uniforms, materials, photographs, and other artifacts. All of these items form a case file that articulates an amazing story of an amazing city protected by an amazing police department.

Since the time of its founding, San Diego's police have been at the forefront of innovation. Our first city marshal later founded the California wine industry. One of his deputies was the first African American lawman west of the Mississippi and served 13 years before the Emancipation Proclamation. Other innovations include a Native American police chief during the 19th century and a female officer before women had the constitutional right to vote.

There has also been tragedy. In one 20-year period, we experienced what was then the largest police gun battle in history, America's worst aviation disaster, the first major school shooting in the United States, and the worst cases of mass murder in history. Unfortunately, the SDPD was not immune to the violence. In that same period, we lost more than a dozen officers in the line of duty and found ourselves with the highest per capita officer mortality rate in the United States.

But bad times never last. The SDPD reinvented itself and is now better prepared for such disasters. Our SWAT team is one of the nation's best, and our per capita officer mortality rate has plummeted.

These are just a few examples of what defines the rich history of the organization. But what makes our history rich are the people who have served the city since San Diego incorporated in 1850.

This is why Ed LaValle and I recruited the SDPD's leaders to write the chapter introductions. This allows the reader to experience firsthand the many different aspects of the department through the commentary of the men and women who oversee it.

Together, Ed LaValle and I share almost 50 years of police experience. As executive board members, we have donated almost a quarter century of service to the San Diego Police Historical Association.

A member of the San Diego Police Department since 1985 and a member of the historical association since 1997, I am also a charter member of the museum and serve as vice president of the board. I have authored two previous books on San Diego Police Department history. With prior service in the California Highway Patrol, Ed LaValle joined the SDPD in 1997 and the historical association in the year 2000; he currently serves as the executive commissioner. We have also authored numerous articles in police magazines about San Diego law enforcement history and the San Diego Police Department.

We hope you find it informative as well as enjoyable.

—Steve Willard

One

DIVERSITY OF PERSONNEL

The San Diego Police Department's annual budget is approximately $400 million. Like most organizations, public or private, success depends on the quality of the people within it.

But here is where we differ: in law enforcement, we are accountable to our community. Unlike private corporations who choose clients, then set hours most profitable for their operations, our mission demands 24 hours a day, seven days a week, and house calls.

Police work anywhere is demanding. In San Diego, it is exacerbated on several fronts. Our Southern Division, along the Mexican border, houses the world's busiest international port of entry. We have one of the largest military presences in the United States, and a steady stream of tourists makes our official population of 1.3 million a remarkably deceptive number.

Despite these unique challenges, we remain one of America's safest big cities, and we have a remarkably clean and efficient police force. Since 1889, one could count on one hand the instances of organized police corruption. And while we have occasionally had rogue officers, they have been dealt with swiftly once we became aware of their activities.

The key to our success is that we only hire the best employees, be it dispatchers, police officers, or support staff. Because we are one of the lowest-staffed per capita police departments in the country, we work hard to give our employees the best equipment, training, and technology the industry has to offer. We then demand innovation and creativity with those resources.

Our standards are high. Only a fraction of applicants will ever serve here, and that is the way it should be. San Diegans have come to accept it. They know that when they call us, they always get a highly trained and professional employee at their door. It has been a standard we have worked exceptionally hard to meet over the past 122 years.

—William Lansdowne
Chief of Police

Before achieving statehood, California was a territory of Mexico. From 1838 until the arrival of American troops in 1845, Antonio Gonzales led a loosely organized group of eight men responsible for keeping the peace in the small, dusty town that would eventually become one of the largest cities in the United States.

When San Diego was incorporated as an American city in 1850, Hungarian count Agoston Harazathy was elected the first city marshal. He made former slave Richard Freeman his deputy, the first African American lawman west of the Mississippi. Harazathy lasted less than two years as marshal, but in that time, he managed to bankrupt the city. He later relocated to Northern California, where he became the founder of the California wine industry.

Judge Roy Bean would be the only man ever held in the city jail. Unable to resist a fight with a cocky San Diego gunslinger, Bean not only shot his opponent, but also the horse he rode in on. Bean later used a spoon to dig his way out of the mud brick jail and headed north. With his 1851 San Diego past well behind him, Bean spent his remaining years in Langtry, Texas, as the "Law West of the Pecos."

With prior experience as both county sheriff and city marshal, the SDPD's first chief, Joseph Coyne, brought a wealth of knowledge to the job. He was not without his critics, however. During the local population explosion of the 1880s, it was common knowledge that the marshal controlled a number of gambling halls downtown. His sidekick in several of his business ventures was none other than famed gunslinger Wyatt Earp.

Chief James Russell is shown with the entire San Diego Police Department in 1897. Despite racially progressive appointments of decades past, personnel within the police department sworn to protecting the community still were not completely representative of it. Except for one Hispanic sergeant, the force was all male and all white.

When Edward "Ned" Bushyhead became the SDPD's sixth chief in 1899, he was a former police commissioner, county sheriff, and the founder of the *San Diego Union*, the region's largest and oldest print newspaper today. Perhaps more remarkable than his distinguished resume, Bushyhead was also half Cherokee Indian, beginning his law enforcement career at a time when a Native American could not testify in a court of law against a white man.

The first man to retire from the SDPD was Sgt. Frank Walter Northern. Hired just months after the SDPD's 1889 formation, Northern was a former deputy city marshal and a civil war veteran when he pinned on his badge. His first night on duty resulted in 17 arrests, six fistfights, and two shootouts.

In 1905, Frank Northern was on patrol alone when he walked up to a warehouse burglary in progress. Officer Northern fought off attackers from every direction before he was ultimately overcome. In 1915, Officer Northern relayed his experience to an artist for a sketch that later appeared in a now-defunct nationwide magazine *Outdoor World*.

Once overpowered, Officer Northern was tied up and placed in a casket. He was then hauled out of town and buried alive in a shallow grave. A band of Native Americans witnessed the burial, rode down, and dug up Officer Northern. The cagey officer commandeered a horse and rode back into town for justice. One of the kidnappers was arrested; the other was hung. The rest of the gang fled town, never to be seen again.

A 1912 *San Diego Sun* editorial cartoon highlights Chief Keno Wilson's cleanup of the vice-ridden Stingaree. After raiding the brothel, prostitutes were put on trains and told to leave town. Madams were ordered to find a new line of work or be jailed. The sweep was reasonably successful; however, it was political suicide. Many city leaders had a financial stake in the seedy district, and it ultimately cost Keno his job. Another tactic would be needed.

14

Det. Reginald Townsend, pictured here in 1915, served only four years, but it was at a time when African Americans were considered less than equal in almost every other profession. Not only did Townsend prove to be one of the SDPD's best investigators, he used health-code violations to finish the cleanup of the Stingaree once and for all. His success was short lived. A 1919 purge returned the SDPD to an all-white, all-male force, and he—along with every other minority officer—was fired.

San Diego had employed a matron as far back as 1905 and a female detective in 1912, but the first policewoman with full powers of arrest was Lucille Jeardue, seen here in 1917. Tasked with patrolling the coastal enclave of La Jolla, Jeardue served at a time before women held the constitutional right to vote.

John Cloud began his 20-year SDPD career as a civilian chauffeur. By the time he retired in 1938, he was the SDPD's first African American supervisor and was overseeing white subordinates. His career took place at a time when the US military and even Major League Baseball, the national pastime, was racially segregated.

Under the direction of Chief Keno Wilson, police clerk William A. Gabrielson started the SDPD Identification Bureau. Stocked with arrest photographs, booking cards, and fingerprints, the bureau quickly grew into one of the largest on the West Coast. Gabrielson left the SDPD and eventually wound up as the chief of the Honolulu Police Department. He was on hand to witness the Pearl Harbor attack on December 7, 1941.

Chief Harry Raymond only led the SDPD for three months; however, his name will forever be linked to a 1937 Los Angeles civic corruption investigation that resulted in the bombing of his car by the LAPD Criminal Intelligence Unit. Raymond survived the blast, and a number of LAPD brass ultimately landed in prison. The bombing ended the career of LAPD chief James Edgar Davis and forced the recall of Los Angeles mayor Frank A. Shaw.

Officer Harry Kay Jr. spent the better part of his SDPD career lecturing the public on traffic safety. He appeared on television and radio and even taught at the SDPD academy for new recruits. Ironically, on March 11, 1957, Sergeant Kay was killed in the line of duty in a single-car rollover.

In January 1957, Officer James J. Washington received the Carnegie Hero Fund Commission bronze medal, a national distinction, for risking his life to pull a citizen from a burning vehicle. One witness to the event said he had never seen such an extraordinary act of bravery. To date, Officer Washington is the only known SDPD officer to ever receive this prestigious award.

Lt. Burl "Dick" Snider was a former US Border Patrol agent assigned to the Southern Division, the command responsible for protecting the border community. His creation of the Border Alien Robbery Force took on the problem of violent crime in the no-man's-land between San Diego and Mexico. The task force proved to be one of the most dangerous in policing history and the subject of a best seller called *Lines and Shadows* by Joseph Wambaugh.

Sgt. Judith Weber's 1990s Western Division patrol squad looks a lot different than any SDPD squad of 100 years before and is much more representative of the community they serve.

Jerry Sanders served the SDPD from 1973 to 1999. He ended his 26-year career after serving six years as chief of police. Sanders returned to public service on November 8, 2005, when he was elected the 34th mayor after Mayor Dick Murphy resigned. The special election marked the second time a former SDPD chief was elected to the highest municipal office in the city.

As the 1990s drew to a close, the world was quickly changing. Among the changes was the need for police advisors in war-torn Kosovo. SDPD detective Vic Shuman and officer Angela Zdunich answered the call for the one-year service, which required a leave of absence. In this December 1999 photograph, Detective Shuman poses in something most San Diegans are not very familiar with: snow.

San Diego police personnel have a tradition of answering the call to war. Since the first officers took a leave of absence to serve their country in World War I, the SDPD has been represented in every armed conflict, sometimes with a heavy price. In October 2008, at 33 years old, Officer Federico Borjas was killed while on a US Army deployment in Afghanistan.

Two

PATROL OPERATIONS

In the SDPD, patrol is the most basic, yet most complex, of all police services. Patrol officers are the "center of the universe"—everyone else plays a supporting role. The patrol division is our most visible element and is our direct communication with the community. Patrol officers usually have less department seniority, but they are often the ones faced with the highest risk, most significant liability, and life and death decisions. That said, being a patrol officer is most likely the SDPD's most rewarding assignment.

Our patrol officers are first responders to crisis situations and critical incidents. We expect them to remain calm, turn disorder into order, and then make split-second decisions that will undoubtedly be scrutinized at a later time. We realize that some of these decisions can ultimately chart the direction for the department, create and/or change the law, direct the future of a chief, or cause political success or failure.

SDPD Patrol Operations includes nine divisions, the watch commander, field lieutenants, Homeless Outreach Team, Beach Teams, and the Headquarters Front Counters. Led by a police captain, each patrol division is divided into service areas comprised of individual communities. These captains report directly to the assistant chief of patrol operations.

In addition to patrol, each division provides investigative and juvenile services to their respective areas. Patrol division detectives handle almost all cases generated by officers; exceptions would include cases assigned to centralized investigations such as homicide, sex crimes, and child abuse. The Juvenile Service Team (JST) provides service to schools within the division's boundaries. Additionally, several commands deploy special teams focused on community issues or specific crime problems. Officers assigned to these teams can work on bicycles, undercover, or on a uniformed crime suppression team.

Today, our patrol officers, investigators, and special team members rely on real-time information to address crime problems. They regularly communicate with each other, centralized investigators, and the department's Crime Analysis Unit to develop strategies to reduce and eliminate crime problems. Patrol operations personnel believes in the concept of intelligence-led policing and utilize contemporary methods to resolving community issues, social problems, and crime concerns. Our officers and detectives work smarter and closer with the community than ever before, creating true partnerships and collaboration with the communities we serve.

—Boyd F. Long
Assistant Chief

The Gamewell system, introduced in 1913, was a remarkable step forward for police communications. The city spent $16,000, a remarkable sum for the time, for a network of call boxes and alert lights placed at strategic locations across the city. A lever thrown at the station activated a flashing light, which alerted a patrolman to proceed to a call box or a pay phone. The system was ultimately phased out in favor of two-way radios.

Before the advent of a two-way radio system, the Emergency Riders of the 1920s were the most efficient way to respond to life-and-death issues. From left to right, Officers Tom Remington, Arleigh Winchester, and Frank Connors sit on their motorcycles outside headquarters awaiting instructions from the desk sergeant as to what emergencies require a police response. Like the Gamewell system a decade before, the Emergency Riders were ultimately phased out in favor of two-way radios.

While police radios are now standard across the United States, they were considered almost science fiction in some parts of the country during the pre–World War II era. Introduced in only five cars in 1932, by the time this photograph was taken three years later in the Balboa Park Police and Fire Alarm Building, the system had already proven its worth.

Officer George Pierce demonstrates the handset receiver of the two-way radio system. The police radio was profiled in a 1939 news story in which Pierce was radio dispatched to an armed robbery, kidnapping, and ultimate slaying of a bank courier. The speed in which information could be sent to officers not only helped Officer Pierce capture the suspects but also resulted in finding the courier's body.

Even in police work, an ounce of prevention is worth a pound of cure. As an officer safety issue, officers should always handcuff their prisoners. This arrestee was compliant all the way up to the jailhouse door, when he apparently had second thoughts about incarceration.

Chief Elmer Jansen (left) meets the fire chief before launching a new police and fire patrol boat in August 1948. Named for former fire chief Louis Almgren, the twin-engine craft was equipped with a high-pressure pump, CO2 extinguishers, radios, and other lifesaving devices. A crew of two manned *Chief Almgren* 24 hours a day. Besides firefighting and lifesaving, duties included patrolling the bay, yacht basin, sportfishing docks, and commercial fishing piers.

24

Lt. Albert Christian, the great uncle of San Diego Police Museum founding member Gary E. Mitrovich, looks on from the far left as uniformed officers and detectives use the street as an impromptu meeting place to share suspect information on a robbery that had just occurred downtown. Working together quickly and efficiently often results in a suspect apprehension.

When the SDPD retired its entire horse patrol at the end of World War II, it was thought that method of policing had seen its last days, but they were wrong. A modified version returned after several people drowned in remote swimming holes in Mission Valley. Because of the remote area, Officer William Derbonne was assigned a mount. This photograph was taken where the Fashion Valley shopping mall now stands.

SDPD officers and a member of the California Highway Patrol (CHP) converge in La Jolla on October 22, 1950, to search for an armed suspect who had just shot a police officer. Why the CHP officer chose to mug for the camera is unknown; however, it is completely inappropriate given the seriousness of the incident.

The first officer on scene usually gets assigned to do the paperwork. The trunk is open, and the evidence kit sits alongside the police car. The officers are most likely inside, looking for clues to a burglary.

An officer conducts a frisk while the sergeant covers the suspects. While such actions would be considered standard tactics in the 1950s, there are a number of safety issues occurring that would deem it unsafe today. Primarily, the suspect's position on the wall affords ample opportunity and leverage to turn and attack the officers.

The SDPD's first police dispatcher, Vernon "Tommy" Thompson, sits at the far left in this photograph. By the time this 1955 image was captured, all SDPD patrol cars were equipped with two-way radios, and the dispatch center, originally staffed with only two people and in operation 18 hours a day, became a 24-hour-a-day, seven-day-a-week operation with civilians and officers working side by side.

Sgt. George Evans works the intake side of the San Diego city jail in this 1955 photograph. From 1889 until the 1970s, the SDPD operated a city jail. Inmates ranged from common thieves to murderers awaiting trial. Overcrowding occasionally pushed the inmate population to more than four times capacity.

Once booked, an arrestee is photographed and fingerprinted. The information is then sent to the records division, where it is catalogued and housed in both a filing cabinet and a punch-card system for fast searches. Such information is valuable for comparing evidence left at crime scenes with known prints and determining an arrestee's criminal history.

Chief of detectives Graham Roland (right) takes time to help the property room officer inventory confiscated weapons in police impounds. As shown in this July 1956 photograph, then, like now, a large number of confiscated items were illegal firearms.

Sgt. A.B. Davis supervises a line of patrol officers as they practice their marksmanship during the summer of 1956. Created in the 1930s with a dedicated range for live ammunition practice, the SDPD's firearms training was considered innovative for the time.

Officers Stan Nevedomski and Jake Koer pose in a 1957 fashion statement most cops would just as soon forget. The hot pink bolo ties were worn in celebration of the Fiesta Del Pacifico, a Balboa Park art event staged to draw more tourists. The ties were not well received by the rank and file. One officer recalled, "I got into more fistfights with catcalling sailors when I wore that tie than in any other time in my career."

Reiterating the danger of wearing a police uniform and being in the wrong place at the wrong time, Officer Herbert Baer recovers from gunshot wounds sustained in January 1958 after he walked into a liquor store robbery in progress. The officer was hospitalized with moderate injuries after the gunman opened fire on him. Officer Baer was able to return fire and kill the robber.

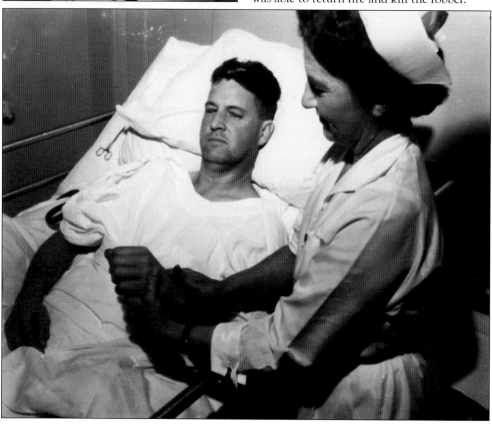

In November 1959, the police department began transferring the majority of its parking enforcement duties to civilian meter maids. In this photograph, taken on their very first day in operation, a priest is blessing the scooters before the maids take to the streets.

A common practice of the early 1960s, the field interview is a procedure still in use today. In addition to keeping track of an individual's crime potential, an officer's documentation of a field contact can help solve crimes and gather vital intelligence.

Sometimes getting out of the police car for even the most basic police work, such as a door check, can yield big results. Unlocked doors sometimes lead to burglaries in progress.

An officer checks his police ambulance equipment at the start of his shift. Prior to the establishment of a paramedic service, the police ambulance was responsible for medical emergency response. In the days before World War II, the SDPD also operated an emergency hospital at each substation. The skills of the police surgeon often meant the difference between life and death. In an era that had not yet heard of a trauma unit, it was a revolutionary idea.

The police ambulance crew was the primary rescuer of two boys trapped in a cave. One of the items available to the crew would have been a Hare traction splint, invented by SDPD officer Glenn "Bud" Hare while assigned to ambulance duty. The enterprising patrolman went on to patent the device, and it sold worldwide, making him a multimillionaire.

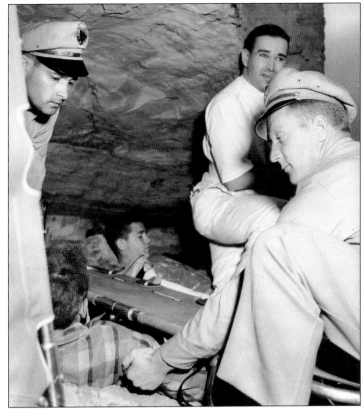

Officer Robert Kravitz takes down a victim's information at the scene of an arson on July 23, 1963. Prior to the establishment of a Metropolitan Arson Strike Team (MAST) in 1980, fire cases were often the most difficult to solve because of the lack of experience officers had in dealing with fires. Placing firefighters on the MAST team to work side by side with detectives has led to MAST being one of the most successful arson investigation squads in the United States.

Great physical evidence always makes a good case. Motorcycle officer Jake Koer (left) and two unidentified patrolmen meet on the patio of the then police headquarters to discuss evidence obtained from an arrest of two armed robbers. The officers have the weapon, the money, and even a change of clothes the suspect used. Note the lack of gloves when handling the gun.

Two uniformed officers are on foot patrol along the boardwalk in Mission Beach in the mid-1960s. Due to ever-increasing violence against officers, helmets were mandatory attire for all uniformed police officers below the rank of lieutenant. Having even the chinstrap unbuckled meant a two-day suspension. The edict was in place from 1963 until 1973.

34

Officers take cover from sniper fire in the southeastern section of San Diego. Civil unrest was rampant across the United States in the 1960s, and San Diego was not immune. At the height of some of the disturbances, officers were assigned to patrol parts of the city with no fewer than three officers per vehicle.

By the 1970s, the SDPD's ambulance service was being disbanded and its duties transferred to the fire department. The back of this ambulance reads, "Tu Seguridad Nuestro Negocio," meaning "Your Safety Our Business," then the official motto of the SDPD. The Spanish version of this motto was placed on only a handful of vehicles assigned to the predominately Hispanic Logan Heights community. It was eventually removed due to the controversy it caused.

By the time this early 1980s photograph was taken of a downtown traffic stop, uniformed female officers had been a part of the police department for almost a full decade. The officers not only wore the same uniforms, they also had the same responsibilities and the same pay. For the time, it was a somewhat unique situation in America.

A canine officer in a bite suit trains takedowns with a police dog. First introduced in 1982 to enhance officer safety, the canine program eventually became the largest police-dog program west of the Mississippi. In 2009, the unit faced the reality of a shrinking budget; a number of officers were cut, and the dogs were retired.

One of the most violent incidents against SDPD officers occurred in Grape Street Park on September 14, 1984. Officers Kimberly Tonahill and Timothy Ruopp were issuing citations to a group for underage drinking. Joselito Cinco, one of the males being cited, suddenly attacked Officer Tonahill and shot her in the torso, knocking her to the ground.

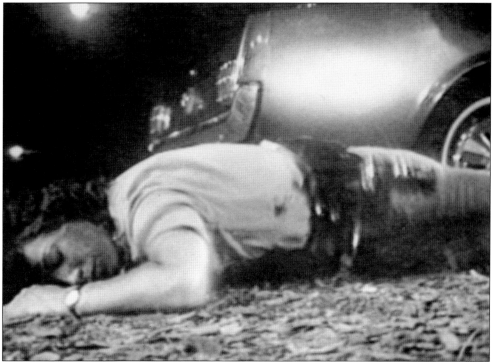

Officer Rebecca Bigbie re-creates the role of Officer Tonahill. A bullet hole can be seen in the side of her uniform shirt. Officer Tonahill was wearing body armor when she was shot, but the bullet traveled between the front and back panel. Immediately after shooting Officer Tonahill, Joselito Cinco opened fire on Officer Ruopp, hitting him multiple times, including what would ultimately be a fatal head wound.

An actor re-creates the role of Joselito Cinco as he fires at Officer Gary Mitrovich. Officer Mitrovich was on patrol several blocks away when he heard Ruopp advise dispatch he would be issuing citations. When he heard the sound of gunshots, Officer Mitrovich drove into the park and saw the officers down. As he exited his vehicle, Joselito Cinco opened fire. Officer Mitrovich was struck in the left shoulder, with the bullet lodging just below his collarbone.

Officer John Tangredi re-creates the role of Officer Mitrovich as he returns fire. Despite being seriously wounded, Officer Mitrovich was able to wound Cinco, then provide responding officers with suspect information and direction of travel. Cinco was later apprehended and sentenced to death. He hung himself in prison in December 1988. For his actions at Grape Street Park, Officer Mitrovich was awarded the SDPD Medal for Valor in 1984 and the Purple Heart in 2010.

Officer Tim Hall tethers an arrestee to his police horse to walk him to an officer with a marked patrol car in this 1980s photograph. While the technique was both humane and effective, it was discontinued after a media photograph caught an African American arrestee, and activists claimed the image was reminiscent of a slave auction.

Introduced in the 1980s, the SDPD's helicopter program is called Air Borne Law Enforcement (ABLE). The officer on the left is the tactical flight officer, and the officer on the right is the pilot. Having the ability to respond anywhere in the city within minutes has been an exceptionally valuable tool for incidents ranging from lost children to suspects at large.

The entire SDPD helicopter unit is flying over San Diego Bay. The ship below them is the USS *Midway*, a World War II–era aircraft carrier that has been converted into one of San Diego's most successful museums.

It is not unusual for police officers to be called on to protect and serve more than just people. When a young California sea lion became lost in Ocean Beach, it sought refuge under the wheels of an SDPD cruiser. SeaWorld San Diego was eventually notified and came to rescue the frightened pup.

Officer Ron Bailiff is at the scene of a man down in the street. Like their predecessors from more than 120 years ago, SDPD patrol officers must be able to respond and adapt to every situation as it unfolds in front of them.

Every May is National Peace Officers Month. San Diego remembers its fallen by having officers and citizens come together for an annual memorial event at the Organ Pavilion in Balboa Park. During the ceremony, the name of each fallen officer is read aloud to the audience. To date, the SDPD has lost the most officers of any San Diego County law enforcement agency.

Three

SPECIAL WEAPONS AND TACTICS

Special Weapons and Tactics (SWAT) was created after the Hub Loan shootout of 1965, a botched pawn shop robbery that saw more than 65 officers trade 1,000 rounds with a lone gunman. Sgt. A.D. Brown eventually entered the building and arrested the suspect after a brief firefight.

Civil unrest in the 1960s led to the formation of the Anti-Sniper Platoon (ASP), a specialized group of three teams of one sergeant and five officers—all volunteers with prior military experience. Weapons and gear came from police impounds. There was no budget or formal training. ASP was never formally used and was disbanded in 1969.

In 1970, the SDPD purchased its first armored step van equipped with chemical agents, weapons, and communications equipment. In support, a new 30-officer SWAT team was created with a budget, special equipment, and regularly scheduled training in 1971.

The 1981 Crandall Street incident, which saw the ambush killing of two police officers, led to the Primary Response Team (PRT). Seven days a week, 24 hours a day, six officers and one sergeant are capable of responding anywhere in the city. Sniper team members who receive ongoing training are an integral component of all PRT SWAT operations. The SDPD sniper team is highly regarded and regularly places among the top in national law enforcement/military competitions.

In 1982, the SDPD pioneered the use of full-time paramedics. Rather than training officers as Emergency Medical Technicians (EMTs), the tactical medical component of SWAT is staffed by full-time paramedics, ensuring the best possible response. The Special Trauma and Rescue (STAR) team attends the SWAT Academy and responds to all emergency calls and training sessions.

The 1984 McDonald's Massacre made it clear that a dedicated hostage rescue team was vital. A Special Response Team (SRT), made up of veteran SWAT officers averaging over 20 years of police experience, soon followed.

Since its creation, SWAT has resolved hundreds of emergencies. Today, the team is equipped with state-of-the-art armored vehicles and the latest in technology, including robots, infrared optics, and the best tactical equipment. Because of the team's capabilities, such as hostage rescue, counterterrorism, dignitary protection, explosive breaching, and numerous other disciplines, San Diego's SWAT unit is ranked as a top-level team by California and national police standards.

—David Ramirez
Executive Assistant Chief of Police

In this 1955 photograph, a lieutenant issues a rifle to a patrol sergeant for use during the shift. Prior to the formation of SWAT, tactical scene response often digressed into a contest of superior firepower. Two major shootouts—one in Mission Hills in 1927 and another in Linda Vista in 1954—led to hundreds of rounds being traded yet no definitive answer on how to better address such issues. It would take the 1965 Hub Loan incident to forever change things.

Officers take cover and a detective returns fire as rounds fly over their heads during the Hub Loan Company shootout of May 1965. The incident began with a botched armed robbery. When it was over, the store owner was dead, and the largest police shootout in US history forever altered how major incidents would be handled.

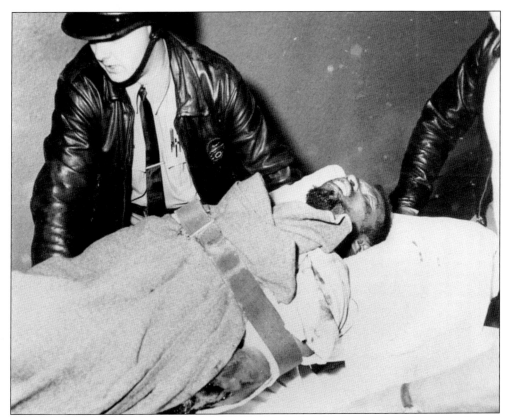

Four hours after it started, the siege was over, but not before the gunman was shot several times with a shotgun. A close look at the suspect's left arm shows significant injuries. Sgt. Allen D. Brown had gone up a flight of stairs and shot the gunman, but not before the suspect tried, unsuccessfully, to shoot Brown with a gun loaded with the wrong ammunition.

Sergeant Brown was the reluctant hero of Hub Loan and the unintended founder of the SWAT team. Local media proclaimed him a hero; however, Chief Wes Sharp dismissed it by saying, "He did what any of my men would have done." Brown later recalled thinking, "Then why didn't they. Why did it have to be me?" In 1984, he was finally awarded the department's highest honor, the Medal for Valor, 10 years after he had retired.

45

An officer of the Anti-Sniper Platoon practices a high-risk entry at an abandoned building at Camp Elliott in the late 1960s.

The SDPD's first SWAT van, introduced in 1970, was primitive compared to what is available today; however, it was a step in the right direction.

Officer Larry Ingraham and agent Gary Evans ended the June 1981 Crandall Street incident at great personal peril. While Ingraham served as the spotter and Evens as the sniper, both SWAT officers had to place themselves directly in the line of heavy gunfire to take out a gunman who was shooting up the neighborhood and had already murdered two police officers.

SWAT officers have to be prepared for any scenario. Fortunately, Stu Segal Productions, a local movie studio that generously provides space for SWAT headquarters, has made a number of sets available for the team to use. In this photograph, SWAT team members gather on a wing as they prepare to enter an airliner.

SWAT officers have to be proficient at rappelling; one slip could result in serious injury or even death. Once again, the Stu Segal movie set provides realistic environments for team members to master the art.

Depending on one's perspective, a sight like this could either be a welcome relief or a sign that the rest of one's life has been planned out by the department of corrections.

A SWAT sniper and spotter take position on a rooftop. Snipers are used not only for active tactical situations but also for major incidents where there is a possibility of rapid loss of control.

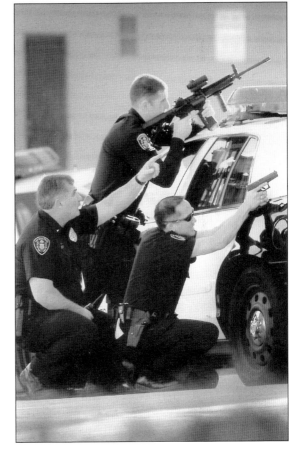

Field commander Lt. Ken Hubbs directs patrol officers towards an open window where a possible gunman is held up. Until a SWAT team can arrive to take over the scene, patrol officers are responsible for keeping things under control.

Much like many other aspects of law enforcement, a successful SWAT mission is rarely achieved by a single person. The hard training, the ongoing regimens, and working side-by-side through dangerous missions make SWAT team camaraderie among the highest of any job in policing.

A far cry from the 1970s SWAT van, the armored Bearcat is well suited for most team missions. With ballistic siding and a gun turret on top, the vehicle can withstand gunfire while safely transporting team members and equipment swiftly in and out of major scenes.

Four

INVESTIGATIONS

The San Diego Police Department employs 330 detectives. Dispersed throughout the department, they work hours that practically mirror uniformed officers. Some are in assignments deemed so critical that they are on call 24 hours a day, seven days a week. Some detectives wear suits and drive vehicles that make them obvious, while others are more subtle. Yet another group of detectives blend with the elements they investigate. How it all began is fascinating.

The need for detectives has always existed; however, it was not until 1907 that the SDPD assigned an officer exclusively to investigative duties. In 1915, the SDPD hired E. Belle Robinson, one of America's first female detectives. She was tasked with investigating crimes against women and children. By 1917, the SDPD required all detectives to be sergeants. Bureau members not already holding that rank were reclassified as investigators or inspectors. Suits and hats were mandatory and remained that way until the 1960s. In 1927, detectives were given specialized duties such as robbery and homicide and assigned to work around the clock.

During World War II, many SDPD detectives assisted the federal government with national security issues within the city. In 1943, the SDPD promoted African American officer William "Bert" Ritchie to detective sergeant. He was one of the first black policemen in America to ever hold such a rank.

In the 1970s and 1980s, the SDPD investigated America's first school shooting, the largest massacre in US history at the time, and a murder that ultimately led to the first execution under a resurrected California death penalty. In the 1980s and 1990s, SDPD detectives not only aggressively worked to reduce the rate of violent crime, they also brought three serial killers to justice. In the 2000s, they handled back-to-back, high-profile cases involving children, including the murder of Danielle van Dam and the disappearance of Jahi Turner. One was solved with an arrest; the other was not.

Today, the department has a lot to be proud of. Despite being one of the lowest-staffed per capita police agencies in the United States, its detectives enjoy one of the nation's highest case cancelation rates. Its success is due to both community cooperation and the excellent caliber of people it employs.

—Cesar Solis
Chief of Detectives

From the 1870s until the early 1920s, San Diego had a major opium problem. This den was typical of many along the West Coast. Primarily occupied by first-generation Chinese, the dens operated mainly in the notorious Stingaree and catered to anyone who had money. While not completely illegal, the dens had a seriously detrimental effect on the quality of life in the district.

Prior to the detective bureau's establishment in 1907, investigations were handled by private investigators paid for by a fund labeled "Secret Service." Despite sharing the name with that of a federal law enforcement agency, there was no relation between the two. The first person selected as an SDPD detective was the large burly man in the center of the photograph, Officer P. Harry Von Den Berg. His investigative responsibilities ranged from truancy to murder. Von Den Berg left the SDPD around 1914. During World War I, he was arrested for being a German spy.

Before computerized fingerprinting, detectives often relied on booking cards. At the bottom of each card was a unique set of numbers and letters called the Henry System Classification Code. The code characterized the fingerprints of the arrestee and could be used to compare against prints lifted at a crime scene, as well as to verify the true identity of arrestees.

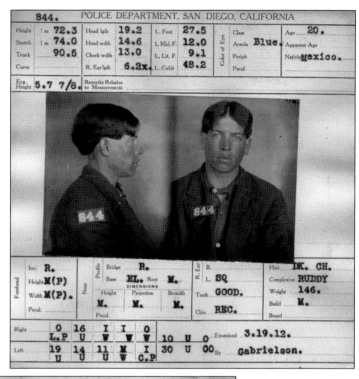

844.		POLICE DEPARTMENT, SAN DIEGO, CALIFORNIA							
Height	1 m 72.3	Head lgth	19.2	L. Foot	27.5		Class	Age	20.
Stretch	1 m 74.0	Head wdth	14.6	L. Mid. F.	12.0	Color of Eye	Areola Blue.	Apparent Age	
Trunk	90.5	Cheek wdth	13.0	L. Lit. F.	9.1		Periph	Nativity Mexico.	
Curve		R. Ear lgth	6.2x.	L. Cubit	48.2		Pecul		
Ear. Height	5.7 7/8.	Remarks Relative to Measurements							

Forehead	Inc. R.	Nose	Bridge R.	R. Ear	B.	Hair	DK. CH.
	Height M(P)		Base EL. Root M.		L. SQ	Complexion	RUDDY
	Width M(P).		DIMENSIONS Height Projection Breadth	Teeth	GOOD.	Weight	146.
	Pecul.		M. M. M.	Chin	REC.	Build	M.
			Pecul.			Beard	

Right	O L.P	16 U	I W	I V	O V		10 U	O	Examined	3.19.12.	
Left	19 U	14 U	11 U	M W	I C.P		30 U	00	By	Gabrielson.	

CANCELLED

CASE NO. A-4346

FORM 111
16-2

DEPARTMENT OF POLICE

HOMICIDE REPORT

San Diego, Cal., May 14 ____ 191 22

Name of person killed __Edw .Dixon__

Residence __Imperial City__

Business __Rooming house proprietor__

Location of homicide __1725 Kearny__

Day, date, hour committed __10.05 P.M. May 14, 1922__

By whom reported __Mrs. Moller__ Address __1725 Kearny__

To whom reported __Sears and Kelly__

Date and time reported __May 14th 10.15 P.M.__

If arrested, by whom _____

Where arrested _____

Witnesses __Mrs. Moller__

DETAILED REPORT

Edw Dixon was shot and killed by John Moller, who then shot and

killed himself.

Today, a murder report is often hundreds of pages long; however, this 1922 report is only two pages long. "Edw Dixon was shot and killed by John Moller, who then shot and killed himself."

53

A motorcycle officer is on crime scene protection duty as detectives sort through evidence at the scene of a 1938 shooting. While the job may not be exciting, it is one of the most important duties in policing. Scene contamination or accidental destruction of evidence can make the difference between an arrest and conviction and the case going unsolved.

A detective points out a bullet hole in the floor at a 1938 shooting scene. Once the photographs are taken, an overall sketch of the scene will be completed. The sketch is a valuable piece of evidence for presentation to a jury.

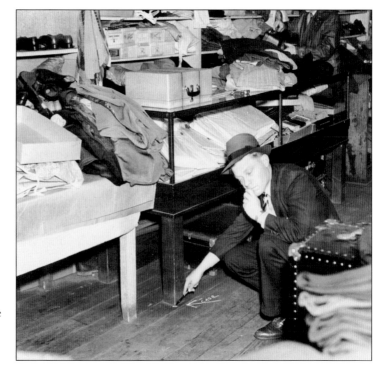

Detectives stand over the newspaper-covered body of a murder victim in June 1938. The cause of the cloud over the coffee table is unknown.

As demonstrated in this August 21, 1944 photograph, domestic violence was then, as it is now, an issue in San Diego. In the 1990s, San Diego was at the forefront of law-enforcement innovation when it became one of the first major police agencies in the nation to create a specific investigative unit to deal with domestic violence.

In January 10, 1945, Det. Sgt. Mike Shea (right) poses on the patio of police headquarters with three seized slot machines. Contrary to popular belief, it is not illegal to own a slot machine in the state of California; the machine just has to be more than 25 years old. In this case, the machines were almost new.

Chief of detectives Graham Roland (left) and a homicide detective watch as a murder suspect demonstrates how he disposed of a body. The reenactment not only helped establish the credibility of the confession but also answered questions as to how the crime transpired from start to finish.

Before the advent of computers, the SDPD's 1940s punch-card machine was a valuable tool. Information was stored in the machine on a stiff piece of paper containing information represented by the presence or absence of holes in predefined positions. Correct use of the machine could save hours in searches for the information needed to build a case.

In this 1940s photograph, homicide detectives are on scene for a body-dump investigation. Good investigative work is about building a case piece by piece while examining every minute detail. With the victim's body nearby, a detective points to what could be a valuable piece of evidence.

A search of the area surrounding the crime scene has located the murder weapon: a military-style .45-caliber pistol. Ballistics can link the casing to a gun; a trace of the gun can lead to the owner.

In an SDPD program intended to cut down on forgery, merchants inked fingerprints of customers using checks in 1947. The program was successful for cutting down on crime; however, it was not popular with the general public. The program was greeted with similar enthusiasm when banks across the country reintroduced fingerprinting in the 1990s.

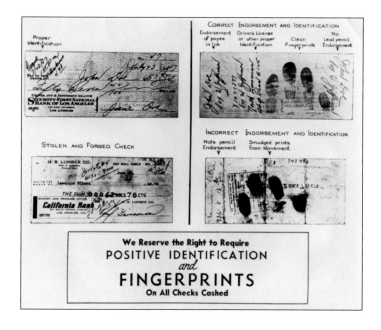

This 1950s photograph shows a grave error in forensics. Movement of crucial evidence, and to do so without gloves, could make this shell casing virtually worthless to an investigation.

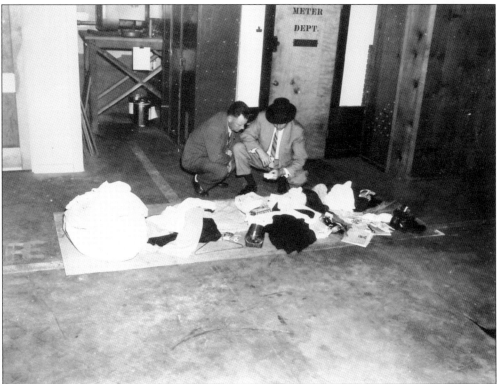

Detectives comb through evidence gathered at a 1950s murder scene. Proper collection is critical to making the case. In order to ensure the highest standards, the SDPD created civilian crime scene specialist positions to handle forensic work at major scene investigations.

A reporter from the *San Diego Union-Tribune* snaps a photograph at a 1950s crime scene. The media can be a double-edged sword. Although very helpful in getting information out to the public, too much information can be detrimental to an investigation or create an overblown public reaction.

The live lineup, often portrayed in television and movies, is perhaps one of the few things entertainment gets correct about detective work. The live lineup is also something still in use today. In this 1955 photograph, witnesses were brought into a darkened room, and suspects were brought to the other side of a one-way mirror. Witnesses then evaluated the line to see if they recognized anyone.

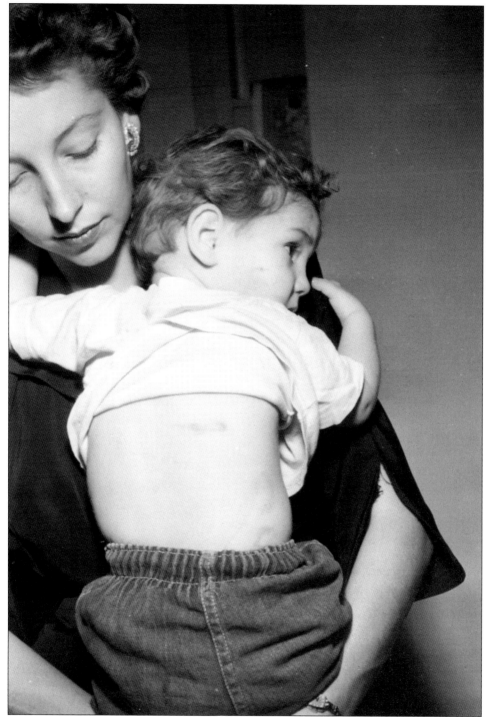

Child abuse investigations are often the most difficult to conduct, even for veteran detectives. SDPD Child Abuse investigates abuse, neglect, and molestation of children under the age of 14. While most detectives quickly admit the emotional challenges, many of them say they find bringing justice to the children more than gratifying.

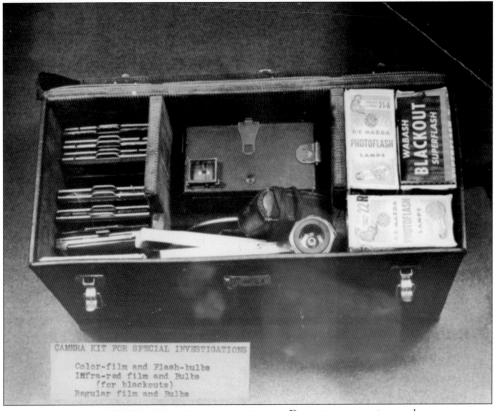

CAMERA KIT FOR SPECIAL INVESTIGATIONS

Color-film and Flash-bulbs
Infra-red film and Bulbs
(for blackouts)
Regular film and Bulbs

Detectives sometimes rely on spy technology to investigate crime. In this early-1960s photograph, the special investigations camera kit is opened up to reveal infrared film and blackout bulbs for undetected photography.

A hidden blackout camera catches a hotel employee using a master key to enter a room and pilfer a coat in this photograph from September 1963. An arrest quickly followed.

Chief O.J. Roed inspects the headliner of a patrol car shot out by a sniper in November 1968. Officers Keith Donahue and J.F. Schmidt were on patrol near 3200 Imperial Avenue when a sniper blew out a side window, missing their heads by inches. An 18-year-old man was later arrested, and the weapon, a high-powered Belgian rifle, was found in his house.

This photograph shows the anatomy of an investigation. From left to right, Detectives Joe Schwalbach and Bob Schroers talk with Officer Larry Kenney at the scene of the crime. Officer Kenney takes the initial report and assists the detectives as needed. Once he is done, the detectives will take what they have back to the office and work as a team to solve it.

Det. Joe Schwalbach uses a graphite brush to dust the counter of the liquor store. Depending on when the counter was last cleaned, he could find hundreds of prints, many overlapping one another. Even if he finds usable prints, the liquor store is a public place, so any suspect would have a legitimate reason to be there. They will still need more evidence.

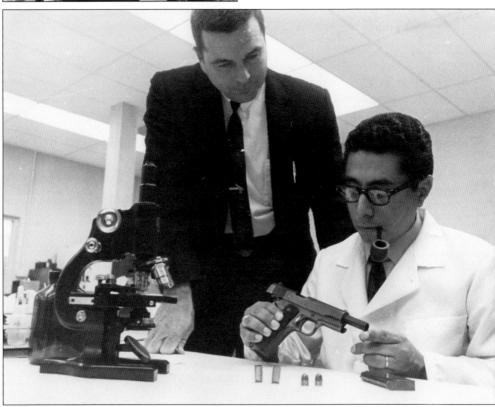

While the rest of his team reviews evidence, witness statements, and other clues, Det. Bert Wright meets with police criminalist Joe Orantes to review the weapon used in the crime. Trained in forensics, Orantes will check the gun for fingerprints and ballistics. Today, it would also be checked for DNA.

Det. Chuck Rucker meets with a witness to complete a composite sketch of the suspect. While officers would never jail someone just for looking like the composite, it will become one more piece in a growing list of evidence to make the case. Due to the limited availability of freehand composite artists in the 1990s, a number of software companies began selling computerized systems that every investigator could easily use.

This meeting with fingerprint officer Jim Roberts will determine what came of the crime-scene prints lifted by Detective Schwalbach. There would be good news: there was a match.

Detectives meet with county coroner Bob Creason, who conducted the autopsy on the victim. A postmortem revealed the cause of death and the time of death, and a bullet was removed from the victim's body. If criminalist Orantes can match the bullet to the gun he is already examining, the team will have another valuable piece of evidence.

Lt. Ed Stevens meets with his detectives to get an update on the case. Once he determines their progress, additional assignments may be needed. In this case, the next step will be to present the case to the district attorney to see if a prosecution can be obtained.

Detectives Joe Schwalbach (left) and Bert Wright meet with Deputy District Attorney Bob Thomas to review the case. Thomas agrees there is enough evidence to file charges once an arrest is made.

An arrest is made, and detectives escort the suspect into the front door of the city jail at police headquarters.

As officers are out making the arrest, Lt. Ed Stevens meets with photojournalist Bob Lampert to prepare a news story.

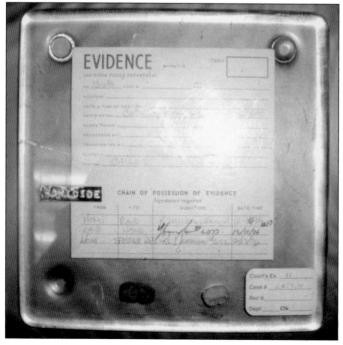

Gum helped solve a December 1976 murder. Detectives, searching the crime scene for evidence, located a piece of chewing gum stuck to a piece of furniture near the victim's body. An examination of the gum revealed a set of teeth prints. Police criminalist and forensic dentist Norman "Skip" Sperber compared the impressions with the bite marks of a possible suspect. It was a positive match. Faced with the evidence, the suspect confessed to the crime.

Officer Kirk Johnson was found dead in his police car in a remote park on February 20, 1983. His headlights were dimmed, and his foot was still on the brake; he had been shot multiple times. A 30-day investigation revealed the suspect to be the 16-year-old son of a deputy sheriff. The boy had stolen his father's uniform, gun, and car and was in the park when Officer Johnson drove up. Faced with arrest, the suspect opened fire.

In one of the largest investigations in SDPD history, a team of officers donned paper suits, grabbed digging tools, and went into the Miramar landfill to look for the remains of little Jahi Turner in May 2002. The two-year-old had been reported missing by his stepfather, who claimed he vanished while in a park. The evidence did not support the story, and detectives suspected foul play. The search turned up nothing, and no criminal charges were ever filed.

The brainchild of former San Diego city attorney Casey Gwinn, the Family Justice Center (FJC) became the world's first one-stop domestic violence resource center when it opened in October 2002. The SDPD took over center operations in 2008, recognizing domestic violence as the number-one motive in San Diego County murders. Today, the FJC is staffed with detectives, lawyers, therapists, and social workers, all dedicated to breaking the cycle of domestic violence once and for all.

Det. Jamal Pasha (in the white shirt and vest) and FBI special agent Ed Cabral negotiate with a despondent Army veteran, possibly suffering from post-traumatic stress disorder, on the roof of a garage. Given the danger if the man landed on his head, the Emergency Negotiations Team (ENT) spent more than an hour talking him down. Staffed with detectives, supervisors, and members from partner agencies, the ENT has call-out responsibilities 24 hours a day, seven days a week. Since their 1976 formation, the ENT has demonstrated a remarkable track record of safe conclusions to very dangerous situations.

Five

WORLD WAR II

The attack on Pearl Harbor sent shock waves across the United States. Outside of Hawaii, no one was affected more than the West Coast.

The SDPD first broadcast the attack to its officers over the two-way police radio at 12:22 p.m. Life in what is now America's finest city would quickly change. Blackouts and rationing would soon be ordered. Officers quickly found themselves under such tight restrictions that they could not drive a police car more than 25 miles per shift. The population of the city would more than double while SDPD staffing was cut by a third. Not long after would come one of America's most shameful acts—Japanese internment.

—Steve Willard

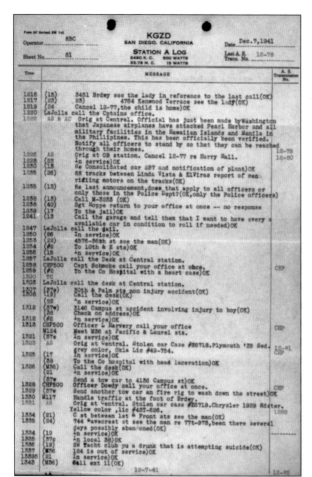

The original radio log from December 7, 1941, announcing the attack on Pearl Harbor shows a quiet Sunday before the attack. Things would never be the same in the days, weeks, and months thereafter. Today, the log is on display in the San Diego Police Museum.

Hours after the attack on Pearl Harbor, Charles Johnson was sworn in as the head of the police auxiliary. His orders: form an all-volunteer police force to augment regular officers being drafted from the ranks. It was the birth of what would ultimately become the police reserve program.

Shortly after the attack on Pearl Harbor, a blackout was ordered across the West Coast. Police cars did not have an exemption, as seen by the blackout lights just above the front bumper. To further compound matters, gasoline was rationed at four gallons per week. Police cars did not have an exemption to that rule either.

Scenes of Cell Block Fire Disaster Fatal to Trapped Prisoners

Five inmates were killed when fire erupted in the San Diego City Jail on February 4, 1942. Fire started at 4:15 a.m. after an inmate attempted to light a cigarette and ignited the cork-lined walls. Men screamed as fire raged through the cells, but because each cell had to be opened by hand, the rescues did not come quickly enough. The jail was later retrofitted with an automatic lever. The fire starter was tried for involuntary manslaughter but was acquitted.

A US Navy ambulance is on scene to help SDPD officers with a crash. It was too late—speeding on rain-slicked University Avenue carried a fatal penalty. In this case, a car lost a head-on collision with a streetcar.

A member of the SDPD Civil Defense tries on a gas mask as part of his training against chemical attacks. The large military presence in San Diego made it an inviting target for the Japanese, so the locals took no chances when it came to preparedness.

As the Zoot Suit Riots raged in Los Angeles during the summer of 1943, San Diego was not without its share of trouble. A number of zoot suiters were arrested for disturbing the peace, curfew violations, and other ordinances. Chief Clifford Peterson snapped this photograph of several of the arrestees before they were escorted to a jail cell.

Chief Clifford Peterson rewards his officers with marksmanship medals. From 1940 until 1947, SDPD officers donned different uniforms. Patrolmen wore the traditional dark blue, while traffic officers elected to move to tan uniforms associated with the California Highway Patrol. The divide was so great that the two even had their own radio frequencies. It was an inefficient way to do business, and to most outsiders it looked as though two different police forces were patrolling the same city.

Camouflage netting covers most of 3100 Pacific Highway, the site of an important bomber factory. From the air, the factory looked like a barren field.

The Axis powers were not the only thing killing US service members during World War II; sometimes, it was simple carelessness. In this case, an Army officer walked between two cars and was struck.

A little creativity in the city jail can lead to comic relief for a serious issue. The "4F" in the booking number was a draft code for a rejected candidate.

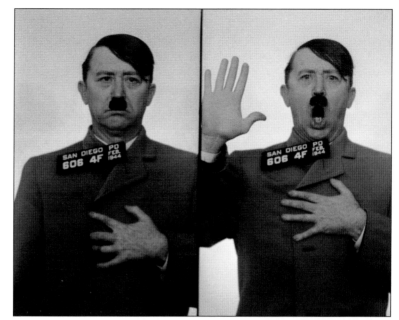

Barrage balloons protect Middle Town, just east of what is now 4000 Pacific Highway. Tethered with metal cables to defend against low-level aircraft attack, some versions of the barrage balloon carried small explosive charges that would be pulled up against the aircraft to ensure its destruction. Barrage balloons were regularly employed against low-flying aircraft. The weight of a longer cable made them impractical for higher altitudes.

Two ranking officers of the auxiliary police sit at a recruiting table on March 27, 1944, to entice additional officers to join. With more than one-third of the regular officers off to fight overseas and the doubling of the local civilian population, men were desperately needed.

The newest additions to the wartime police auxiliary pose with their brand-new badges, patterned after a silver six-point ball-tip badge worn by SDPD officers of the early 20th century. Modern SDPD historians originally surmised these smaller shields—one of which resides in the police museum—were a short-lived version, worn between 1900 and 1905.

Even with war raging overseas, there was still crime to fight in the city. On October 16, 1944, officers on patrol at the bus station opened up Paul Abatya's suitcase and discovered it was full of heroin.

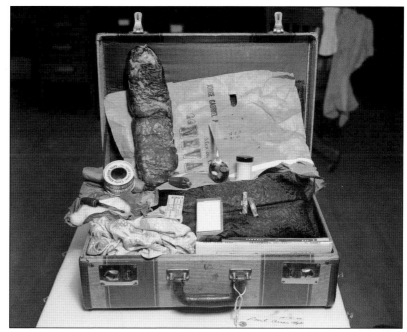

A November 1944 photograph of Horton Plaza shows downtown teeming with activity. The ticket office for the professional football team, the San Diego Bombers, can be seen in the foreground of the iconic 1910 fountain.

Smoke from a November 22, 1944, PB4Y-2 military plane crash billows from a hill in Loma Portal. Responding officers will have to deal with death, a dangerous fire, and a curious crowd. The cause of the crash was later determined to be 98 missing bolts and a wing only attached with four pins. A coroner's jury ultimately found Consolidated Vultee guilty of gross negligence and ordered the company to pay $130,484 to the families of six dead crew members.

Only one SDPD officer and a handful of firemen are now on-scene at the plane crash. While the military will have the ultimate responsibility for the investigation and clean up, the curious mob coming down the hill is an issue needing immediate intervention. Military personnel, armed with rifles and bayonets, will keep the crowd at bay.

Six

SPECIAL OPERATIONS

The SDPD is organized into four operational areas: Patrol, Special Operations, Centralized Investigations, and Neighborhood Policing. When officers have reached the pinnacle of their patrol achievements, many aspire to other assignments: enter Special Operations.

Special Operations covers diverse assignments supporting patrol and investigations throughout the city. Additionally, it provides strategic management of critical incidents that allows officers to be equipped with the best resources. It is made up of Traffic, Air Support, Event Development and Management Unit, Operational Support, Canine, Critical Incident Management/Homeland Security, SWAT/SRT, and Fleet Safety.

Traffic (AIB) is tasked with investigating injury collisions, driving under the influence (DUI) enforcement, vehicle code and traffic-related municipal code enforcement, and traffic-related matters such as evaluating street safety conditions and making engineering recommendations. Traffic officers receive extensive training on accident investigations and typically become court-certified experts. The motorcycle unit requires its officers to undergo a highly competitive selection process and then complete a rigorous two-week academy. They are a vital component of traffic, tasked with vehicle and municipal code enforcement. Additionally, Motors, the official name of the unit, conduct accident investigations and support AIB.

Traffic Special Events Operations manages all permitted special events within the city, staffed by sworn officers and civilian Special Event Traffic Controllers (SETC). Parking Enforcement manages parking-related issues citywide and is staffed by Parking Enforcement Officers (PEOs).

Air Support (ABLE) provides aerial support for police operations 24 hours a day, seven days a week. Currently, there are two fixed-wing aircraft and four helicopters in the fleet. From the air, ABLE can safely take over pursuits when they become too dangerous on the streets. ABLE also provides an aerial overview of critical incidents and has led to many successful resolutions that otherwise might have involved injury to officers or civilians.

One premier unit within the SDPD is the SWAT team. Executive assistant chief of police David Ramirez covered their mission in chapter three. The Canine Unit is world-renowned for its innovation and success. The officers are highly trained and manage dogs trained in general, narcotics, and evidence searches.

All told, Special Operations works closely with patrol, investigations, and neighborhood policing to provide the highest level of service to all of San Diego.

—Lawrence McKinney
Assistant Chief of Police

Chief Peterson sews a Traffic Division patch onto the sleeve of Sgt. Karl Sprague. Introduced around 1940, only traffic officers with advanced accident-investigation skills were allowed to wear the patch, which was discontinued in the late 1940s. In 2006, a replica of the patch hit the market; however, the red-and-white color scheme was wrong, as the correct colors are blue and white. Today, both the real patch and incorrect replica are valuable collector's items.

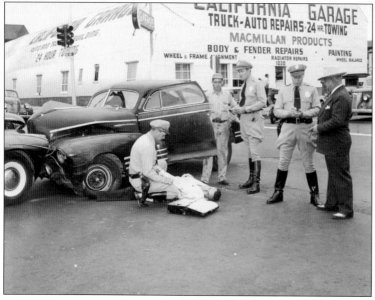

SDPD traffic officers are on-scene for a serious injury accident in the intersection of Tenth Avenue and G Street on June 11, 1948.

Created as an educational tool in the early 1940s, the Death-O-Meter was displayed at the front counter of police headquarters and updated on an as-needed basis. The meter kept track of each traffic-related injury and fatality. While the subject matter was grim, the numbers clearly indicate that traffic injuries were a serious issue and safety education was necessary.

It is a fact that no one likes getting a traffic ticket; however, studies have shown verbal warnings alone do not often work. In this July 13, 1948, case, the violation is for speeding across the Laurel Street Bridge in Balboa Park.

Shortly after World War II, the police department began an aggressive campaign to educate the public on the dangers of careless driving. Billboards sponsored by private companies began to appear across town trying to educate the public about a very serious problem. The campaign worked. Despite an increasing population, traffic deaths began to show a decline across the city.

Police officers are not immune to dangerous driving. In this case, a vehicle pulled into the path of a police motorcycle, sending the officer over the hood. With little more than a pair of leather gloves serving as his safety gear, it is a miracle the officer was not killed. Other motorcycle officers have not been as fortunate. Since 1915, almost a half-dozen SDPD motorcycle officers have been killed by vehicle collisions.

To aid in the fight against pedestrian-versus-vehicle deaths, especially those involving children, a school safety-patrol crossing guard was brought in to help control busy intersections. To ensure people obeyed stop signs, occasionally black-and-white patrol cars were assigned to the intersection as well.

SDPD officers conduct a DUI checkpoint. While the issue was a hotly contested debate in the 1990s over search and seizure, the SDPD had been successfully using checkpoints from as far back as 1938.

Carelessness cost a bicyclist his life. A city truck was turning into the operations yard at Twentieth and B Streets when a young man was speeding down a large hill on his bicycle from the east. The impact drove the cyclist under the truck with serious head trauma. He died at the scene.

Traffic duty can be a stomach-churning experience. A corpse lies between two motorcycle officers as they watch a patrolman search the wreckage of a vehicle for possible survivors.

Traffic duty is more than just citations; there is also an investigative end. In this 1950s case, a detective searches for clues to a hit-and-run on the bumper of a possible suspect vehicle.

Officers assist at the scene of a fatal crash along Highway 101, just south of Del Mar city limits.

A traffic officer adjusts his car-mounted radar unit prior to hitting the streets. While it was a tremendous technological advancement for the 1960s, today the radar is outdated and has been replaced by a much more accurate laser.

On August 19, 1972, Officer Tom Giaquinto became the last sworn San Diego police officer to work parking enforcement on a three-wheeled Servi-Car motorcycle. Today, parking enforcement is performed by civilian parking-enforcement officers.

Seven

COMMUNITY POLICING

San Diego's crime rate is at its lowest in nearly half a century, and it now ranks among the safest cities in the United States. Much of the credit goes to the SDPD's tremendous partnership with the community.

In the late 1980s, the SDPD was awarded a Bureau of Justice Assistance grant to demonstrate the effectiveness of Problem Oriented Policing (POP), a concept of using data and analysis to determine how to best reduce crime. Capt. Jerry Sanders (San Diego's current mayor) dedicated a team of officers to tackle violent crime in a specific, gang-ridden area of the southeastern division. The success of the project launched citywide neighborhood policing.

Patrol officers waded into the vast elements of crime and began to systematically tackle problems, working shoulder to shoulder with community groups and residents. Results were dramatic: crack houses dried up, prostitutes left, graffiti was abated, and the crime rate dropped. Several programs were either enhanced or produced along the way, including crime prevention through environmental design (CPTED) and situational crime prevention (SCP). Through community partnerships, officers became experts at identifying and solving problems.

The entire department was then trained in neighborhood policing methods. To support these efforts, the department created one of the largest and most successful volunteer programs in the country. These volunteers play a vital role in the department's vision to engage the community in a problem-solving partnership to reduce crime and positively affect the quality of life in each of the city's communities. Today, more than 700 volunteers donate more than 150,000 hours annually, and it is considered a national model for other police departments.

In addition to volunteers, the SDPD assists with more than 950 neighborhood watch groups. Officers at all ranks routinely attend more than 170 community meetings each month. This is in addition to the many community events attended each weekend. Department accessibility has never been greater because of the outreach throughout our city. No area goes untouched, and the police officers are a welcome part of every community.

—Shelley Zimmerman
Assistant Chief

When the City of San Diego annexed the community of San Ysidro more than 50 years ago, it inherited what is now the world's busiest port of entry. The department also inherited a need for officers to better understand other cultures within the area they police. Today, the SDPD is at the forefront of policing and has established liaisons and trust within almost every community it serves.

When tobacco pitchman Johnnie Roventini came to visit police headquarters in 1939, Officer Oscar "O.W." Ericson made sure to get into the photograph. At the time, the 48-inch-tall Roventini was internationally known and commanded a salary of more than $20,000 per year to shout his famous line "Call for Philip Morris!" during radio-show commercials. While this photograph was just for fun, it could be a violation of police department policy prohibiting product endorsements today.

Every year, the San Diego County Fair is held at the Del Mar fairgrounds, and every year, the SDPD responds with an exhibit. This elaborate 1948 set highlights the history of the police department. Today, many of the items seen in the photograph reside in the San Diego Police Museum and are much more protected.

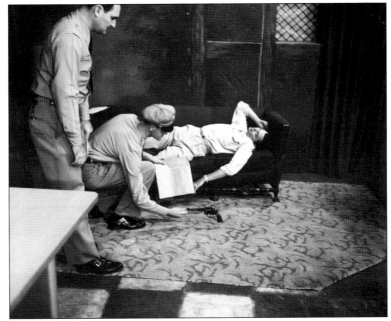

A dead body on the couch and a gun on the floor might indicate a suicide. Here, the 1950s television show *Information Police* conducts a reenactment showing how officers would respond to such an incident. The person on the sofa is an actor.

Sometimes, there is a lot more to being a police officer than just putting bad guys in jail. In this photograph, a crowd of children looks on as two uniformed officers participate in a three-legged race; the officers lost.

If a police department is going to be representative of the community it protects, its best recruits will come from within the community. This 1960s traveling exhibit was used at police headquarters open-house events, the Del Mar fair, and any other public venue that could attract quality applicants.

Officers Alberto Puente and Chuck Rucker are pictured outside a community-relations storefront during the 1960s. The community storefronts played a vital part in breaking down barriers in communities that might not otherwise go to a police station. The offices were easily accessible and nonthreatening. Unfortunately, as city budgets began to shrink, many of these storefronts fell victim to the fiscal axe.

As the 1960s drew to a close, it was becoming painfully obvious some communities did not trust law enforcement. In this image, Lt. Ken Fortier meets with ministers and reverends from the southeastern section of San Diego in order to establish trust and communication between the SDPD and surrounding communities. Not only was the program a resounding success, other departments were soon using it as a model for similar programs in their cities.

Officers Aaron Graham (left) and Roger Owens get back to the roots of policing and walk a foot patrol beat in downtown San Diego in the 1970s. Many police historians surmise police community relations took an almost-fatal hit with the introduction of the police car, because it made beat officers faceless and unapproachable. While response times are a lot slower on a foot beat, the activity level of a good foot-patrol officer can be very high.

Officer Tim Hall stops to allow a man and child to pet the police horse in the mid-1980s. Like the foot patrolmen, police horses are a bit old-fashioned; however, they are always a huge community-relations hit. The horses served their purposes for canyon patrol and crowd control at large events as well. In 2009, the horse patrol was eliminated due to budgetary constraints.

Eight

THE CRIME LAB

The San Diego Police Department has a long established history of innovation, and the crime laboratory is no exception. From humble beginnings, the laboratory has always been on the cutting edge of forensics, breaking new ground in efficiency, analytical techniques, database utilization, and automation.

In 1939, Chief George Sears designated a vacant room at police headquarters to house a municipal police crime laboratory, which was somewhat of an anomaly for its time. The laboratory opened with a couple of employees, a few donated microscopes, a darkroom, and other basic items for evidentiary examinations. Analysts working in the laboratory were generalists, experts in all areas of forensics.

Today, the laboratory has 70 employees and offers seven areas of analysis. Laboratory personnel process crime scenes and provide crime-scene reconstruction services. Highly educated scientists now work exclusively in their areas of expertise, including latent prints, firearms, DNA analysis, chemistry, trace evidence, polygraph, and documents.

Technology has also advanced. Once requiring a visible amount of blood to achieve results, current criminalists are able to extract DNA off items of evidence that have merely been touched. Instrumentation can be mounted in the back of patrol cars to test DUI drivers roadside, providing immediate results. Glue tanks, magnetic powders, and electrostatic lifting allow analysts to obtain prints from virtually any surface. Fingerprints, DNA profiles, and cartridge case markings are entered into national databases and compared to other cases all over the country. Automation has improved efficiency so significantly that even with 16,000 requests in 2011, the laboratory is able to offer analytical services for all types of cases, from homicides to burglaries.

In a world of increased robotics, more sensitive testing, and the challenges of dwindling budgets, the nationally and soon-to-be internationally accredited SDPD crime laboratory remains on the forefront of efficiency and technology as it continues serving the citizens of San Diego.

—Jennifer Shen
Crime Laboratory Director

By the 1920s, the SDPD Identification Bureau had grown from just a few print cards into a giant repository of dozens of cabinets full of information.

In this 1930s murder investigation, the handgun on the dresser is an exceptionally vital piece of evidence; however, the reflection of the cameraman in the mirror is distracting. Because all crime-scene photographs taken must be developed and checked into evidence regardless of quality, this photograph was eventually shown to a jury.

Lt. Walter Scott (right) demonstrates how to use clear tape to lift fingerprints off glass in this 1940s photograph. The credit for the creation of the SDPD crime lab belongs to several people, but most importantly Chief George Sears (who authorized it), Lt. Walter Scott (who led it), and Det. Sgt. William "Bert" Ritchie (who helped obtain most of the equipment for it).

In this image, a 1940s crime lab employee uses the photostat machine. Invented in 1907, the large machine was the first photographic copy machine in the world. A prism was placed in front of the lens to reverse the image. After a 10-second exposure, the paper was directed to developing and fixing baths, then ether-dried. The result was a negative print that took about two minutes to produce, which could, in turn, be photographed to make any number of positive prints.

Chief of Police Elmer Jansen (left) gets a lesson in the workings of some of the lab's newest equipment in the 1950s.

The fingerprint files held the inked cards of every person arrested in the city of San Diego since 1910. Each set of prints was classified according to type—arches, loops, and whorls—and then entered into a coded filing system. When an unknown print was lifted at a crime scene, a print specialist could search the file for similar prints and then make a direct comparison. The process was very labor intensive.

Primarily equipped with cameras, microscopes, and a few pieces of vacuum tube-powered equipment, the lab of 1947 would be primitive by today's standards.

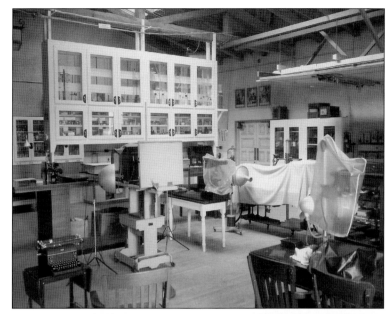

When school administrators at Roosevelt Junior High School discovered a safe burglary on June 9, 1947, lab personnel were called to the scene. Photographs were taken and prints were lifted. The dial was burned off by an acetylene torch stolen from the school metal shop. Two juveniles were eventually arrested.

While the last half century has seen significant advances in forensics, one technique that remains relatively unchanged is a basic search for latent fingerprints. A black graphite powder and brush can reveal with 100 percent accuracy if a person has been at a crime scene. In the case of an August 20, 1947, commercial burglary, the prints are high quality and easily identifiable if there was a known suspect. The advent of computers significantly sped up the search process.

Lieutenant Scott demonstrates a low-power microscope to a group of academy officers on September 10, 1956. The more new officers can learn about forensics, the more likely they will be to properly preserve and collect evidence when they encounter it.

Det. Harry Clunn is connected to a polygraph machine while Sgt. Bob Prouty runs the test. Pioneered within the SDPD by Lt. Bob Karrow in the 1950s, lie detectors are not admissible in court; however, they still serve a valuable purpose. In addition to requiring all police applicants to undergo a polygraph examination, detectives can test the credibility of individuals in questionable cases. This photograph was taken as part of a training exercise in the 1960s.

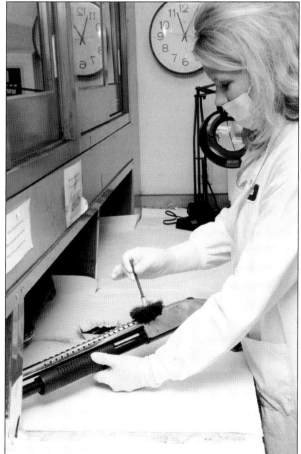

While today's SDPD crime lab is one of the most modern municipal crime laboratories in the United States, some evidentiary processing techniques remain relatively unchanged. In this case, a crime-scene specialist uses the age-old technique of a print brush and graphite powder to process a shotgun for fingerprints.

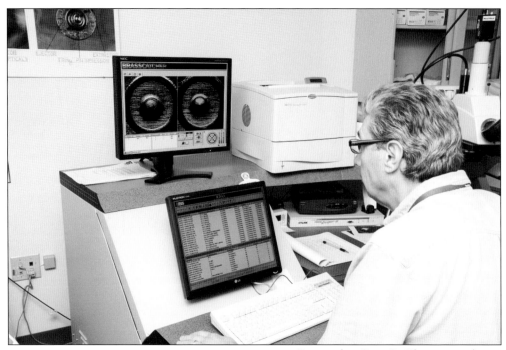

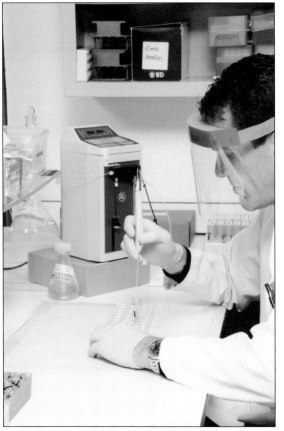

Criminalist Gene LaChimia matches miniscule marks left on a discharged shell casing to that of a known weapon. This type of ballistics test will determine if this specific gun was used in the crime detectives are investigating. With the advent of networked computers, criminalists can now check files across the United States to see if the gun is wanted in connection with a violent crime in another jurisdiction.

The use of DNA for police investigations was first reported in 1984 by Sir Alec Jeffreys at the University of Leicester in England. Within 10 years, the SDPD became one of the first police laboratories in the United States to embrace the technology as part of its investigative procedures.

Nine

DEFINING EVENTS

How the San Diego Police Department came to be known as "America's Finest" is as evolutionary as it is revolutionary. Of course, many of the advances the SDPD has made are due to routine advancement of time—things simply evolve. There have also been times where innovative members of the police department recognized a need and then devised a way to fill it.

Other issues have forced the police department to adapt or suffer. Some events, such as the crash of PSA Flight 182 and the McDonald's Massacre, have been so large that not only were they first-time defining events for the SDPD, but other law-enforcement agencies around the United States looked to the SDPD for answers about preparedness in handling similar situations within their communities.

—Steve Willard

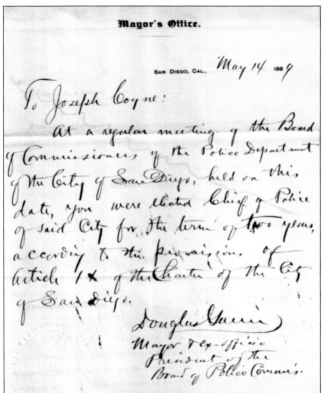

Mayor's Office.

San Diego, Cal. May 14, 1889

To Joseph Coyne:

At a regular meeting of the Board of Commissioners of the Police Department of the City of San Diego, held on this date, you were elected Chief of Police of said City for the term of two years, according to the provisions of Article IX of the Charter of the City of San Diego.

Douglas Gunn
Mayor & Ex-Officio
President of the
Board of Police Comm'rs.

Without a starting point, there would be no SDPD. That is why one of the most defining events in department history is a single piece of paper now residing in the police museum. It is the document that started it all: the letter from Mayor Douglas Gunn informing Joseph Coyne he had been selected as San Diego's first chief of police on May 14, 1889.

Jack Whyte is trying to incite a riot in front of the San Diego city jail on February 25, 1912. The crowd gathering is part of the national Industrial Workers of the World (IWW) movement and was set on creating havoc in San Diego. Whyte was soon arrested and charged with two counts of criminal conspiracy. The uprising was far from over.

More protesters were arriving daily. With the jails rapidly filling with members of the Industrial Workers of the World, also called "Wobblies," just trying to contain the peace was a major challenge; it was exactly what the organizers had planned.

A city jail can only hold so many people, so when the jail population surged to tens of times over capacity, the police department began housing arrestees in pens along Pacific Highway. They still had no solution to deal with the waves of Wobblies who were coming into town.

Police turn the water cannon on IWW protesters to break up a crowd in downtown San Diego. By now, protests had been occurring for such a length of time, the SDPD was starting to crack. More than a quarter of the department had resigned, and those left behind were stuck working 18 hours a day, seven days a week, to deal with the unrest. The *San Diego Union* blasted Chief Keno Wilson for using excessive force when they turned the hoses on the protestors.

Arrests, fire hoses, and even temporary jails were not working. The only thing left to do with the Wobblies was to send them back from whence they came. Train stations were flooded as police marched or delivered protesters in paddy wagons. Before the protesters were put on the train, a vigilance committee severely beat them and added an admonition to never return. The tactic worked.

Special officers wore powder-blue uniforms for the 1915 Panama-California Exposition in Balboa Park. If the event was to put San Diego on the map, it needed to be safe. The special contingency of officers wore uniforms patterned after the Spanish military. The yearlong event was so successful, it was continued for another year. While some officers transitioned into the SDPD and served full careers when the exposition finally ended, others were laid off and took jobs in the private sector.

During the flood of 1916, the level of Lower Otay Reservoir rose more than 27 feet in 10 days, Morena Reservoir rose 17.5 feet in the same period, and Upper Otay filled in three days. The dam in Switzer Canyon had to be dynamited, as it had been cracked and weakened. Bridges across the city were wiped out, and roads were underwater. The coroner's office estimated 50 people died; later estimates have placed casualties at around 20.

Officer Arleigh Winchester (left) and California Highway Patrol (CHP) officer Leslie Ford inspect a cash courier's Cadillac that was shot up by two men armed with machine guns on May 20, 1929. The loss in the robbery murder was $80,000 in cash—the drop from the Agua Caliente Racetrack in Tijuana. The getaway car was located in Golden Hill, and blood was found inside. One of the triggermen had been shot in the crossfire. Detectives soon closed the case with the arrest of two ex-convicts from Los Angeles.

Orchestrated by protesters from Los Angeles, an event began on May 30, 1933, in Pantoja Park against FDR and Wall Street, ultimately erupting into one of San Diego's largest riots ever. In this photograph, things have gotten out of hand. Officers waded into the crowd throwing fists after several protesters began desecrating the flag.

The tide turned when officers fired tear gas into the crowd. In the end, nine people were arrested. Nine policemen and 30 protesters went to the hospital. The *San Diego Sun* later opined, "The disgraceful riot could have been prevented. Had the agitators been permitted to march peacefully, nothing would have happened. Fanatical as they may be with respect to the best way of curing our social ills, these young men and women [had] the right to convene and parade."

As with 20 years prior, the SDPD kept the peace at another Balboa Park event, the California Pacific International Exposition, in 1935. A new uniform was introduced: dark blue with an over-the-shoulder, Sam Brown–style duty belt. While officers were able to keep crime to a minimum, they upset city leaders by seizing gaming equipment from an exhibit hall set up as a casino. Chief Sears responded, "The last time I checked, gambling was just as illegal north of Broadway as it is south of Broadway."

Chief George Sears stands to the far right in the photograph to provide not only a welcoming committee but also security to Pres. Franklin D. Roosevelt. The president was on hand to dedicate a new civic center at 1600 Pacific Highway in 1938. The city would eventually deed the building over to the county when it moved to a modern building at 202 C Street in the early 1960s.

May 9, 1939, marked the 50th anniversary of the SDPD, as well as the opening of a brand-new, 90,000-square-foot police headquarters at 801 West Market Street. In addition to its aesthetically pleasing design and construction by master architects, for the first time in the history of American policing, a police headquarters incorporated all police functions, including training, lab, dispatch, administration, corrections, motor pool, and patrol all under one roof.

This 1939 photograph shows police headquarters from the intersection of Pacific Highway and Market Street. The building was made to last for generations; however, its ultimate downfall became its size, as it ultimately proved to be too small for a rapidly expanding city. The expansive lawn in the foreground was among the first things to go. It was paved over to make way for additional parking. By the 1980s, the area was filled with trailers doubling as office space.

The end of World War II opened a Pandora's box of labor discord across America. Over the next 18 months, labor and management slugged it out across picket lines in almost every industry; San Diego was no exception. In this photograph, employees of one of San Diego's largest employers, Consolidated Vultee, protest outside of SDPD headquarters as part of a 101-day strike. Enough officers were assigned to monitor the protest that it remained nonviolent.

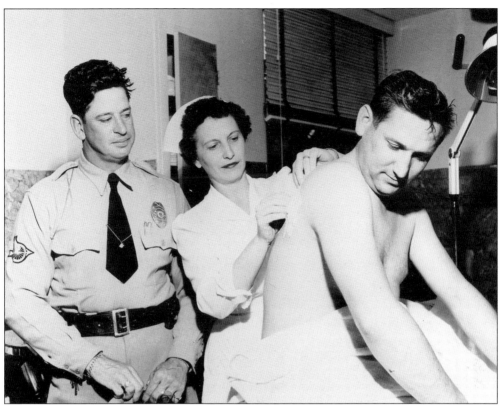

Officer John "Irish" O'Neil watches as a nurse treats Det. John Zemcik, who was shot while attempting to save Deputy Marshal Elwin Bunnell. The marshal had walked into a trap set by a man with a shotgun and took a round to the stomach. Zemcik was shot while trying to pull him to safety. Officers quickly surrounded the house and traded hundreds of shots with the gunman, making the 1954 incident one of the largest gunfights ever. The suspect was later convicted of attempted murder.

Victor Olsson (on the floor) snuck into the headquarters squad room and disarmed the police range master on November 1, 1958. As he was preparing to execute him, patrolman Chuck Rucker walked by a window. Rucker bolted to another window where he had a clean shot, then took it. Olsson's last words were "I'm sorry." Ironically, the range master had been chastising Rucker to update his marksmanship qualifications. In appreciation, Rucker was awarded a lifetime exemption from future requirements.

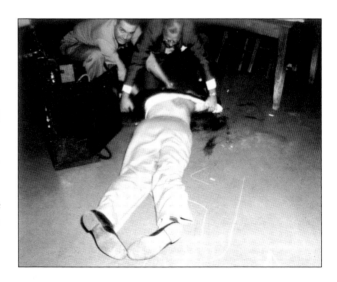

San Diego firemen battle an August 1965 blaze in a neighborhood market after a teenager threw a Molotov cocktail inside. The incident was part of San Diego's first race riot and was related to the Watts riots in Los Angeles that began on August 11. In the San Diego riot, 65 were arrested, but only 4 people were hurt. Property damage was moderate.

Chief Ray Hoobler uses a public-address system to command a group of rioters to disperse from the streets of Ocean Beach in a 1968 civil disturbance. Originally, Hoobler had instructed his officers to remain behind him. Several minutes later, the officers began to get pelted with rocks and bottles. Hoobler personally led the charge into the group, where dozens of arrests were made.

Antiwar sentiment was at a fever pitch across the United States. Even with the massive numbers of officers present, this 1972 downtown protest wound up getting out of hand when protesters stormed onto the freeway and spilled into city hall.

What began as a peaceful antiwar protest at city hall quickly turned violent and moved into the core of downtown. As rioters became more out of control, officers formed a protective ring around the American flag in order to protect it from being burned.

Members of the Border Alien Robbery Force (BARF) attend a 1976 briefing before a night in the violent no-man's-land of canyons dividing Mexico and San Diego. The BARF experiment lasted less than two years and put a huge dent in the nightly attacks against undocumented immigrants, but it came at a price: the task force was one of the most dangerous and violent assignments in the history of American policing.

BARF team members lay in wait for bandits. While this team donned uniforms, members also occasionally dressed as migrants to serve as decoys for the bandits. The canyons were dark, cold, and unforgiving. Fortunately, no SDPD officer lost his life during the operation.

With the hills of Tijuana as the backdrop, a US Border Patrol helicopter provides illumination for a takedown of suspected bandits. Due to the officer safety issues, the BARF team was eventually replaced by a better-equipped, all-uniformed team of US Border Patrol agents and SDPD officers.

Pacific Southwest Airlines (PSA) flight 182 was inbound from Los Angeles shortly after 9 a.m. on September 25, 1978, when it was struck by a Cessna 172 over North Park. Both planes plummeted to the ground. County photographer Hans Wendt was covering an outdoor press conference when the planes collided. He pointed his camera towards the sky and captured this remarkable photograph.

Ground zero of the PSA crash was near the intersection of Dwight and Nile Streets. The bulk of the debris fanned out towards Boundary Street. The explosion created a mushroom cloud that could be seen for miles. A total of 144 people were killed, an additional nine people on the ground were injured, and 22 homes across a four-block area were destroyed or damaged. At the time, it was the most deadliest commercial air disaster in America. It remains the worst in California's history.

On January 29, 1979, 16-year-old Brenda Spencer leaned out her bedroom window with a .22 rifle and opened fire on Cleveland Elementary School across the street. Two school employees were killed, and eight children were injured in the incident. An SDPD officer was also shot trying to perform a rescue. Later, when asked why, Spencer responded, "I don't like Mondays." In 1980, the Boomtown Rats released a single titled after the phrase. Some radio stations found the song so offensive, they refused to play it.

Officers evacuate the wounded after James Huberty walked into a south San Diego McDonald's restaurant and opened fire on July 18, 1984. More than 20 people were killed and an almost equal number wounded before a SWAT sniper ended the carnage. Less than 30 minutes earlier, Huberty had told his wife, "Society's had its chance. I'm going hunting—hunting humans." At the time, the incident, later dubbed the San Ysidro Massacre, was the worst case of mass murder in American history.

Det. Sergeant Alberto Leos (left) has a unique perspective on the massacre—he was a 16-year-old cook inside the McDonald's and was shot multiple times attempting to save two coworkers. Severely wounded, Leos crawled to the basement and used his shoelaces as tourniquets. He spent 1985 learning to walk again. Nine years later, Leos joined the SDPD. In 1995, he was awarded a lifesaving medal after pulling a man from a burning car. (Photograph courtesy of Arnie Reyes.)

Officers Kevin Ammon and Mo Parga conduct an arrest at 5000 Logan Avenue during the Walking Enforcement Campaign Against Narcotics (WECAN), a mission designed to address the gang and drug violence that drove San Diego's murder rate to an all-time high in 1988. The project of aggressive policing, targeting known gang members in areas with high rates of violence, was so successful that WECAN later morphed into the Gang Suppression Team (GST), a unit that still exists today.

SDPD employees gather on the patio of police headquarters to celebrate the 100th anniversary of the police department in May 1989. Despite the fact the city population has increased by hundreds of thousands of residents in the last 22 years, the department had roughly the same number of sworn officers in 1989 as it does today.

In one of the wildest police chases ever, on May 18, 1995, Shawn Nelson raced through city streets in a stolen Army tank. The 57-ton machine obliterated everything in its path. The chase ended with Nelson stuck on a freeway divider. Officers rushed the tank as Nelson shifted the gears back and forth. He was fatally shot after refusing to surrender. Property damage was extensive, but other than Nelson, no one was harmed. (Photograph courtesy of Tom Keck.)

With the Biotech conference headed to town in June 2001, the SDPD prepared for the worst. Two years earlier, Seattle police had dealt with some protests that escalated into violence, and the subsequent rioting left parts of their downtown in shambles. Determined not to let the same thing happen in San Diego, a mobile field force began training in riot deterrence and mass arrests. Fortunately, they were not needed; an overwhelming police presence on the street kept protesters calm.

When seven-year-old Danielle van Dam was kidnapped from her bedroom in an upscale neighborhood in February 2002, an international media frenzy quickly followed. Neighbor David Westerfield, a 50-year-old computer programmer with no criminal history, quickly became the focus of the massive investigation. With an arsenal of evidence against him, Westerfield was ultimately convicted of her kidnapping and murder and sentenced to death. Ironically, in 1949, Westerfield's father also made headlines when he was arrested as part of a San Diego burglary series.

In October 2003, and again in October 2007, the city of San Diego was met with massive wildfires. As there were not enough firefighters to go around, sometimes officers—in this case, Det. Dee (Cirino) Massey—grabbed a garden hose and helped where they could.

During the fires, some of San Diego's most vulnerable citizens also needed rescuing: pets. Local animal shelters pitched in to help and took in many stray dogs, cats, and even horses and other exotic pets.

Air quality during the fires became so poor, Sgt. Ray Stachnik's team of officers were forced to don air masks to continue working. In both fires, the flames were extinguished long before the air quality improved.

At first glance, this may appear to be a scene from a war and a bombed-out street, but it used to be an upscale neighborhood. Sgt. Mark Van Abel (pointing) directs Detectives Holly Erwin (left), Dee Massey, and Steve Skinner to other locations where they may be needed.

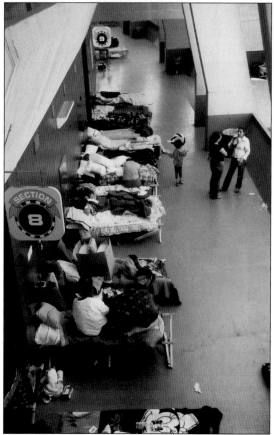

With thousands of citizens evacuating their homes, there needed to be somewhere for them to go. Qualcomm Stadium was one of the only places in the city large enough to house everyone who had been dislocated. While it was safe from the flames, the setup was not exactly comfortable.

Even though 95 years had passed since Officer Emery Campbell became the first killed in the line of duty, the museum staff had no idea which badge he wore. It was not visible in the only known photographs of him, and badge no. 47 had a compelling story, as did no. 48. In 2008, DNA finally revealed the answer. Despite the ravages of time and frequent polishing, a microscopic speck of blood was found on the pin catch of badge no. 48.

Sometimes, what is most important never makes the headlines. In this 2009 photograph, Chief William Lansdowne applauds his newest officer, Ryan Herdman. Sworn in as an officer for the day, the eight-year-old boy was facing terminal brain cancer. He later rode in a police car, helicopter, and boat. Herdman recounted that it was the best day of his life. He passed away less than two months later. His remains were provided a police escort to the celebration of his life.

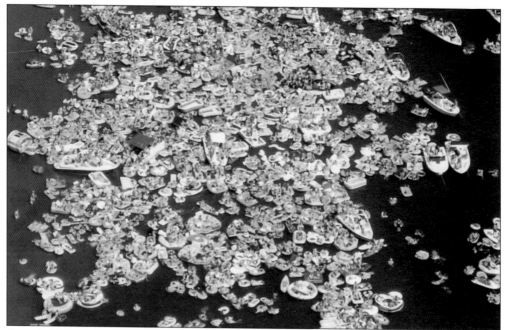

Some 2,500 residents gathered on the water in September 2009 to protest a city council ban on alcohol on city beaches. Because a loophole in the law allowed alcohol to be consumed as long as feet were not touching the sand, a flotilla of rafters paddled several feet offshore to drink. Officers were on hand, but few problems were reported. The council followed up with a more comprehensive ban, effectively ending the flotilla forever.

One of the largest gatherings of police cars in San Diego history occurred in the Qualcomm Stadium parking lot in September 2010 as officers set the stage for the funeral of Officer Christopher Wilson, who was shot and killed in the line of duty on August 28, 2010. Unfortunately, the scene was repeated in the same parking lot less than a year later to memorialize Officer Jeremy Henwood, who was killed after an individual drove up next to his patrol car and opened fire with a shotgun.

In remembrance of the 10th anniversary of the 9/11 attacks, the authors designed an SDPD-authorized, optional badge for the month of September. Named San Diego County First Responders United, the badge symbolized the continued unity of local emergency service, and for one month, it was also an optional insignia for almost all police and many fire agencies across the county.

DISCOVER THOUSANDS OF LOCAL HISTORY BOOKS
FEATURING MILLIONS OF VINTAGE IMAGES

Arcadia Publishing, the leading local history publisher in the United States, is committed to making history accessible and meaningful through publishing books that celebrate and preserve the heritage of America's people and places.

Find more books like this at
www.arcadiapublishing.com

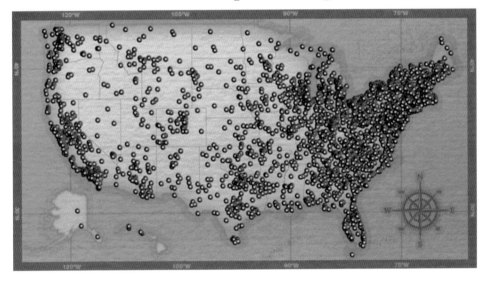

Search for your hometown history, your old stomping grounds, and even your favorite sports team.

Consistent with our mission to preserve history on a local level, this book was printed in South Carolina on American-made paper and manufactured entirely in the United States. Products carrying the accredited Forest Stewardship Council (FSC) label are printed on 100 percent FSC-certified paper.

MADE IN THE USA